Table of Contents

Introduction

This book is primarily for those interested in learning to write simple programs or games for the Panic Playdate in the Lua programming language using a Mac OS or Windows computer. You might be able to use this book for development on a Linux computer, but the steps may be different, and familiarity with Linux is necessary. This book will cover drawing lines, rectangles, circles, text, basic sprites, playing sounds, using buttons and using the crank, simple animation and using tilemaps. More advanced topics, such multiple sprite collisions, writing files, etc. will require referring to the Panic Playdate documentation or other references.

I decided to write this book because I prefer to read a guide to doing something instead of watching a video. The information in this book comes from a number of sources, such as the Playdate SDK documentation and the Playdate developers forum, but I thought it would be convenient to have everything in one place to refer to for producing sounds on the Playdate, or drawing sprites,using tilemaps or using fonts (the Tic Tac Toe program uses fonts).

It is possible to have shorter programs, especially for some of the games and tilemap programs, by using object oriented programming. So some of the programs may not be the most elegantly written, but may be more readable for what is happening in the code. There may be a second book that is more object oriented, depending on the interest and demand for it.

Disclaimer of liability

No warranty is made on software in this book. The reader assumes responsibility when making use of code found in this book. The code in this book was tested with the Playdate SDK version 2.6.2. It is possible that updates to the SDK version may cause some code to require modifications. The author will attempt to update the book as time permits and an update is feasible.

Usage of code in this book

You are welcome to use the programs in this book, and you can make use of my code if you produce your own game or other program (in a significantly modified form). For the link to download the programs in this book, see chapter 14.

Where to go for help

Playdate has a developers forum at:

https://devforum.play.date/

There is a search button on the upper right that you can click on to search for a topic you need help with. I found a lot of useful information here when writing this book.

If you do not see an answer, you can create a developer forum account and even post new threads.

Copies of the .PDX files of some of the programs in this book will appear at:

https://arhtur.itch.io/

If you have purchased this book and have difficulty implementing something similar to some of my programs, I may be able to help. From time to time, I might check my itch.io page for comments and respond as time permits. You can post a comment to one of my programs with any relevant questions.

Downloading and Installing the Playdate SDK

Downloading the Playdate SDK (software development kit)

The first step is to download the SDK. Go to:

https://play.date/dev/

and download the correct SDK for your computer platform and install the SDK.

Setting up the SDK

For the latest documentation, refer to:

https://sdk.play.date/2.6.2/Inside%20Playdate.html

When compiling your code, you can manually call the Playdate compiler, or you can use an IDE (integrated development environment). One IDE, called Nova (for MacOS), offers a 30 day free trial, but after that, costs $99 for a year of updates. Visual Studio Code (VS Code) can be used. In Windows, there is a useful template for Visual Studio Code.

Windows setup

In Windows, there is a useful template for Visual Studio Code made by user SquidGodDev. This template only has instructions at the Github website for setting up Visual Studio Code for Windows or Linux. You can find it here, with instructions on how to set it up:

https://github.com/SquidGodDev/playdate-template

I found 2 things to watch out for when using the above playdate-template with Windows 11.

This is assuming you have followed the set up instructions in the above link. Visual Studio Code should be restarted after setting any environment variables. Also make sure you have installed the Lua and Playdate Debug extensions in Visual Studio Code.

First, make sure that the Documents folder you are using is consistent between the

Playdate SDK installation, the Visual Studio playdate-template-main and the settings of your PLAYDATE_SDK_PATH environment variable. Windows 11 has this OneDrive cloud Documents folder that can be confusing. I found it helpful to create a local Documents folder shortcut in Windows File Explorer.

Second, when opening the playdate-template-main folder in Visual Studio Code, make sure you are not opening the top playdate-template-main folder, or when building, you will get an error message. You have to go to Visual Studio Code and select File->Open Folder and open the second playdate-template-main folder (within the top playdate-template-main folder).

If you have difficulty setting up Visual Studio Code, another option is to manually compile your .LUA files at the command prompt and manually open the simulator.

Here is a useful link for compiling Lua project on Windows for the Playdate:

https://devforum.play.date/t/tutorial-compiling-lua-projects-on-windows/3332

If you have a file main.lua to compile, you should be able to type pdc main.lua
If that doesn't work, you can specify the SDK path with:

pdc -sdkpath c:\Users\Username\Documents\PlaydateSDK main.lua

If pdc cannot be found, then the PLAYDATE_SDK_PATH has not been set up correctly.

Mac OS setup

You can use Nova or Visual Studio Code or Textedit on Mac OS to edit your .lua files. If you are using Textedit, go to Settings and for Format, select Plain Text instead of Rich Text. Also disable Check Spelling as you type and disable Check spelling automatically.

Opening the Terminal Window (on Mac OS)

To open a terminal window, go to Finder and click on **Applications**. Then click on **Utilities** and then **Terminal**.

Specifying the SDK path on Mac OS

For Mac OS, there are 2 ways to specify the path to the SDK. One is to always put it when using the Playdate compiler (pdc). For example when compiling main.lua pdc -sdkpath ~/Developer/PlaydateSDK main.lua

You can also edit the .zshrc file. The easiest way might be to use the vi (visual editor). You can Google search "using vi" for more information. In the .zshrc file, the Playdate website says to add:

```
export PLAYDATE_SDK_PATH=<path to SDK>
```

Where <path to SDK> is your path to the Playdate SDK, usually something like:

/Users/USERNAME/Developer/PlaydateSDK

You must replace USERNAME with your username for your Mac OS computer.

Introduction to Lua and coding for the Panic Playdate

This chapter goes over the basics of Lua. If you are familiar with another programming language, you might be able to skip some of this chapter.

For Panic Playdate programs, there is a directory structure they use. You might want to create a separate directory for each program. For example, from the PlaydateSDK directory, make a new subdirectory (or folder) called testprograms, and then a subdirectory in testprograms for each program you make.

The pdxinfo file

Here is some important information about the pdxinfo file. This is described in section 4.6 of the Playdate SDK documentation. Below are the contents of an example file, which is place in the same location as your code, such as main.lua

name is the name of your program.
imagePath is the path for the images to icon.png and card.png

The icon.png file is a 32x32 pixel icon that shows up in your list of Playdate device games. card.png is a 350x155 pixel image that you see if you sideload the program from the Playdate website. See the chapter at the end of the book for loading programs onto the Panic Playdate.

Extremely important is the **bundleID**. For every program, this must be unique. I keep the com.arhtur part the same and change the last part (program1 in this example).

version is the version of your program.

```
name=PlaydateProgram
imagePath=SystemAssets
bundleID=io.itch.arhtur.program1
version=1
```

Lua Exmaple 1 - print

For your first program, open a new file in your text editor or IDE.

Type the following and save it as main.lua:

```
print("hello world")

function playdate.update()
end
```

Go to the terminal (or command prompt) and type:

pdc -k main.lua

If that command doesn't work, you might need to specify the path of the SDK:

pdc -sdkpath ~/Developer/PlaydateSDK -k main.lua

This will make a file called main.pdx

To use the Playdate Simulator, you can either use Finder (or Windows Explorer) and double click on main.pdx

You can also open the Playdate Simulator and select File and Open … and open main.pdx

You might need to open the Simulator console window, by clicking on **Window** and selecting **Console**

In the console window, you should see **hello world**

By the way, on the Panic Playdate hardware, you won't see this message. For that, you will need to use the playdate.graphics.drawText command.

Lua Example 2 - print a number

In this example, you can print a message with a number to the Playdate screen.

The statement **import 'CoreLibs/graphics.lua'** is necessary to use the drawText command

We use **gfx=playdate.graphics** so that we don't have to type playdate.graphics for every graphics command.

The **drawText** command has 3 arguments: text,x-location,y-location

In the **drawText** command, we use .. to print the text and the value of the variable a.

And finally, we always need the playdate.update function which is continuously called (so we don't want to put a drawText command in there, or it will be called repeatedly.

Here is the whole program:

```
import 'CoreLibs/graphics.lua'

a=3

gfx=playdate.graphics

gfx.drawText("the number is "..a,0,0)

function playdate.update()
end
```

Lua Example 3 - if statement

In Lua, the syntax of the simple if statement is:

if condition then
  true code
end

In this code, you will see the message "a is 5"

Notice that when we set a to 5, we use one equal sign = and when we compare if a is equal to 5, we use the double equal sign ==.

```
import 'CoreLibs/graphics.lua'

a=5

gfx=playdate.graphics

if a==5 then
  gfx.drawText("a is 5",0,0)
end

function playdate.update()
end
```

Here are some possible ways to compare numbers in Lua:

Equal to	==
Not equal	~=
Less than	<
Less than or equal to	<=
Greater than	>
Greater than or equal to	>=

Lua example 4 - if then else statement

Sometimes you might want to execute a different branch of code if the if statement is not true.

The syntax is:

if condition **then**
  true code
else
  false code
end

In this example, you will see the message "**a is not 5**"

```
import 'CoreLibs/graphics.lua'

a=3

gfx=playdate.graphics

if a==5 then
  gfx.drawText("a is 5",0,0)
else
  gfx.drawText("a is not 5",0,0)
end

function playdate.update()
end
```

Lua Example 5 - if statement with and condition

Sometimes we want to test if two conditions are true. In Lua we use the **and** condition.

Here is an example with that:

```lua
import 'CoreLibs/graphics.lua'

a=3
b=7

gfx=playdate.graphics

if a==3 and b==7 then
  gfx.drawText("a is 3 and b is 7",0,0)
end

function playdate.update()
end
```

Lua Example 6 - if statement with or condition

If we want to test if one condition or another is true, we use the **or** condition. In this example, a is 3 and b is 7. Since one of the conditions is true, you will see "**a is 3 or b is 5**"

```
import 'CoreLibs/graphics.lua'

a=3
b=7

gfx=playdate.graphics

if a==3 or b==5 then
   gfx.drawText("a is 3 or b is 5",0,0)
end

function playdate.update()
end
```

Lua Example 7 - if statement with not equal

To test if something is not equal we use **~=**

In this example, you will see "**a is not 5**"

```
import 'CoreLibs/graphics.lua'

a=3

gfx=playdate.graphics

if a~=5   then
  gfx.drawText("a is not 5",0,0)
end

function playdate.update()
end
```

Lua Example 8 - for loop

To repeated do some code for a set number of times, we use the for loop.

The syntax is:

for variable=start,end,step do
  loop code
end

In this example, we display the numbers 1 to 10

```
import 'CoreLibs/graphics.lua'

gfx=playdate.graphics

for a=1,10,1 do
  gfx.drawText(a,0,a*20)
end

function playdate.update()
end
```

Lua Example 9 - for loop counting backwards

In this example, we will count down from 10 to 1 by using the following for loop:

for a=10,1,-1

Please note that when drawing the text, we must use (10-a)*10 for the y location.

Here is the code:

```
import 'CoreLibs/graphics.lua'

gfx=playdate.graphics

for a=10,1,-1 do
  gfx.drawText(a,0,(10-a)*20)
end

function playdate.update()
end
```

Lua Example 10 - while loop

Sometimes we don't know when we want to stop a loop, so we use a while loop. The syntax is:

while condition **do**
  loop code
end

This time, we are printing the numbers from 2 to 20, counting by 2's across the screen.

When using a while loop, care must be taken that an exit condition is true at some point. Otherwise, the program might be stuck in an infinite loop and you might have to quit the simulator.

Here is the code:

```lua
import 'CoreLibs/graphics.lua'

gfx=playdate.graphics

a=2

while a<22 do
  gfx.drawText(a,a*10,0)
  a+=2
end

function playdate.update()
end
```

Location of files for this book

For the location of files in this book, please refer to this link:

https://tinyurl.com/plaadayt27182

Please do not post the link or related files, since considerable effort has been made to produce these programs and this book. As stated at the beginning, you are welcome to use the programs, and you can make use of my code if you produce your own game or other program (in a significantly modified form).

Program 1 - sketch program

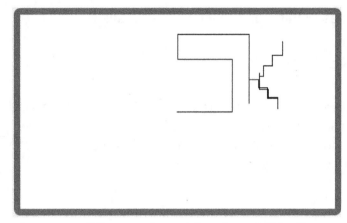

This first program makes use of the crank and the A and B buttons.

Before the actual code, I will explain functions used for the buttons and crank.

When the A button is pressed the function playdate.AButtonDown() is called.

Here is an example function that prints "A button is pressed" to the console.

```
function playdate.AButtonDown()
  print("A button is pressed")
end
```

For the B button, the function playdate.BButtonDown() is called.

For the crank, it is necessary to import 'CoreLibs/crank'

We call playdate.getCrankTicks(ticksPerRevolution), where ticksPerRevolution specifies how many crank ticks we want to detect. A smaller number like 6 means 6 ticks are generated for one clockwise revolution, and one tick for every 60 degree movement. One counterclockwise revolution will generate -6. A larger number like 360 means 360 ticks will be generated for one clockwise revolution.

The following example will print to the console window how many ticks were detected. We have to use the if statement

if crankTicks~=0

or else many print messages will be generated, even when the crank is not being turned.

```
import 'CoreLibs/crank'

function playdate.update()
  local crankTicks = playdate.getCrankTicks(6)

  if crankTicks~=0 then
    print(crankTicks.." ticks detected.")
  end
end
```

Now, onto the sketch program. When the program is run, turning the crank will draw horizontally. If you press the A button, it will switch to drawing vertically. The B button clears the screen with gfx.clear()

In the function playdate.AButtonDown(), we use the mod (%) operator. The mod function calculates the remainder when dividing. For example, 1 mod 2 is 1, because 1 divided by 2 has a remainder of 1. 2 mod 2 is 0 because 2 divided 2 has a remainder of 0. The mod function is a fast way of ensuring that the value of modes is either 0 or 1.

We use the **gfx.drawLine(x1,y1,x2,y2)** function to draw the lines.

In Lua, if you see – (two dashes) it means a line with comments, and that line is ignored when the program is compiled.

The download file name is **sketch.zip** at my download link.

```
--sketcher
--copyright 2024 R. Tanikawa

import 'CoreLibs/graphics.lua'
import 'CoreLibs/crank'

gfx = playdate.graphics

modes=1

dx=200
dy=120
```

```
--*********************************

function playdate.AButtonDown()
  modes=(modes+1) % 2
end

--*********************************

function playdate.BButtonDown()
  gfx.clear()
end

--*********************************

function playdate.update()
  local crankTicks = playdate.getCrankTicks(100)

  if modes==1 then
    nx=(dx+crankTicks)
    if nx<1 then nx=1 end
    if nx>399 then nx=399 end
    gfx.drawLine(dx,dy,nx,dy)
    dx=nx
  else
    ny=(dy+crankTicks)
    if ny<1 then ny=1 end
    if ny>239 then y=239 end
    gfx.drawLine(dx,dy,dx,ny)
    dy=ny
  end
end
```

Program 2 - music with Bach Minuet in G

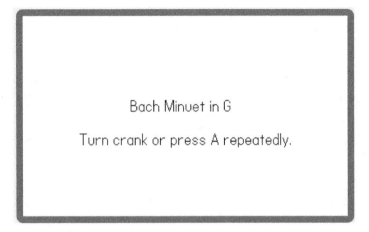

Bach Minuet in G

Turn crank or press A repeatedly.

To play sounds on the Playdate, first make a variable snd which is playdate.sound

local snd = playdate.sound

The first thing to set is the wave type with the synth.new() function. I like to use a triangle shaped wave. The synth.new() function returns a synth object.

s = snd.synth.new(snd.kWaveTriangle)

The Playdate uses the ADSR model to generate sounds. Each part has a time duration. Here is a table explaining that:

Attack	Amount of time for sound to reach full volume.
Decay	Amount of time for sound to decay from full volume to the sustain level.
Sustain	Amount of time note is held at the sustain level, until release.
Release	Amount fo time for the note to fade to zero after it is let go.

Almost every instrument has these values, from pianos, to guitars and trumpets. Not all of the parameters need to be set. Here are some settings I like:

```
s:setDecay(1)
s:setSustain(1.2)
s:setRelease(2.5)
```

To play a note with MIDI (musical instrument digital interface), you can call playMIDINote("C4") which would play the C note in the 4th octave. After playing the note, you must call the function noteOff(). I store the notes to the Bach Minuet in G in an array. In Lua, arrays are accessed, starting from index value 1. You must keep track of the last array element, so that when you reach it, you can go back to element 1 to avoid having the program crash.

The download file name is **musicBach.zip** at my download link.

```lua
--Bach Minuet
--implementation copyright 2024 R. Tanikawa

import 'CoreLibs/crank'
import 'CoreLibs/graphics'

gfx=playdate.graphics

local snd = playdate.sound

m=1

ar4={"G4","C4","D4","E4","F4","G4","C4","C4","A4","F4","G4","A4","B4",
"C5","C4","C4",
"F4","G4","F4","E4","D4","E4","F4","E4","D4","C4","D4","E4","D4","C4",
"B3","C4",
"E5","C5","D5","E5","C5","D5","G4","A4","B4","G4","C5","A4","B4","C5",
"G4","F#4","E4","F#4","D4","D4","E4","F#4","G4","A4","B4","C5","B4","A
4","B4","D4","F#4","G4",
"G4","C4","B3","C4","A4","C4","B3","C4","G4","F4","E4","D4","C4","B3",
"C4","D4",
"G3","A3","B3","C4","D4","E4","F4","E4","D4","E4","G4","C4","B3","C4"

}

s = snd.synth.new(snd.kWaveTriangle)
s:setDecay(1)
s:setSustain(1.2)
s:setRelease(2.5)
```

```
gfx.drawText("Bach Minuet in G",133,100)
gfx.drawText("Turn crank or press A repeatedly.",70,140)


--**********************************

function playNote()
  s:playMIDINote(ar4[m])

  m+=1
  if m==95 then
    m=1
  end
  s:noteOff()
end


--************************************

function playdate.AButtonDown()
  playNote()
end


--**********************************

function playdate.update()

  local crankTicks = playdate.getCrankTicks(4)

  if (crankTicks~=0) then
    playNote()
  end
end
```

Program 3 - Shape drawing

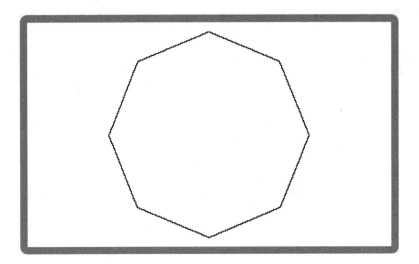

This program can draw polygons from 3 to 20 sides. I made a function called draw1(cval) which has an input cval, the crank value. Negative values decrease the number of sides and positive values increase the number of sides.

To draw shapes we use the math.cos() and math.sin() functions. These trigonometry functions do not use degrees, but radians, so we must take an angle and multiply by math.pi and divide by 180. We calculate the angle ang by taking 360 degrees and dividing by the number of sides. We use a for loop with counter m, where m is based on the number of sides.

To center the polygon, we add 200 to our x value and 120 to our y value (the screen resolution of the Playdate is 400x240). We have to multiply by 110 to fill most of the screen.

x=200+110*math.cos((m-1)*ang*math.pi/180)
y=120+110*math.sin((m-1)*ang*math.pi/180)

The download file name is **shape.zip** at my download link.

Here is the entire program:

```
--shapes drawing
--copyright 2024 R. Tanikawa

import 'CoreLibs/sprites.lua'
import 'CoreLibs/graphics.lua'
import 'CoreLibs/crank'
import 'CoreLibs/timer'

gfx=playdate.graphics

sides=3

--***********************************
function draw1(cval)
  sides+=cval
  if sides<3 then
    sides=3
  end

  if sides>20 then
    sides=20
  end

  gfx.clear()
  ang=360/sides

  for m=1,sides,1 do
    gfx.drawLine(200+110*math.cos((m-1)*ang*math.pi/180),
      120+110*math.sin((m-1)*ang*math.pi/180),

200+110*math.cos(m*ang*math.pi/180),120+110*math.sin(m*ang*math.pi/180
))
  end
end

draw1(0)

--***********************************
```

```
function playdate.update()

  local crankTicks = playdate.getCrankTicks(6)

  if crankTicks~=0 then
    draw1(crankTicks)
  end

end
```

Program 4 - Dice roll

The Dice program takes advantage of certain patterns for the dice dots to reduce the code size, according to the table below:

Number(s)	Action
Odd numbers	Draw center dot
2, 3, 4 and 6	Draw bottom left and upper right dots
4, 5 and 6	Draw upper left and bottom right dots
6	Draw 2 dots on middle row

Turn the crank to roll or roll again.

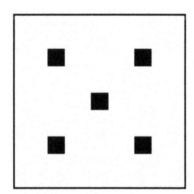

The download file name is **dice.zip** at my download link.

```
--dice
--copyright 2024 R. Tanikawa

import 'CoreLibs/sprites.lua'
import 'CoreLibs/graphics.lua'
import 'CoreLibs/crank'
import 'CoreLibs/timer'

local snd = playdate.sound
gfx=playdate.graphics

s = snd.synth.new(snd.kWaveTriangle)
```

```
s:setDecay(0.5)
s:setSustain(0.6)
s:setRelease(0.5)

--***********************************

function roll()
  sz=12
  gfx.clear()
  gfx.drawRect(120,35,175,175)
  dice=math.random(6)
  if (dice % 2)==1 then
    gfx.fillRect(200,121,sz,sz)
  end
  if (dice>1) then
    gfx.fillRect(156,164,sz,sz)
    gfx.fillRect(247,71,sz,sz)
  end
  if (dice>3) then
    gfx.fillRect(247,164,sz,sz)
    gfx.fillRect(156,71,sz,sz)
  end

  if (dice==6) then
    gfx.fillRect(156,121,sz,sz)
    gfx.fillRect(247,121,sz,sz)
  end
end

roll()

--***********************************

function playdate.update()

  local crankTicks = playdate.getCrankTicks(200)

  if crankTicks~=0 then
    if math.abs(crankTicks)>4 then
      roll()
```

```
        s:playNote(110)
        s:noteOff()
    end
  end
end
```

Program 5 - Fortune ball

A "fortune telling" ball can be made by generating a random
number and printing various messages based on the number. In
this case, one of 5 messages will be printed. Turn the crank or
press the A button for another message.

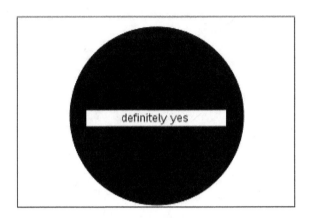

The download file name is **fortune.zip** at my download link.

```
--fortune ball
--copyright 2024 R. Tanikawa

import 'CoreLibs/sprites.lua'
import 'CoreLibs/graphics.lua'
import 'CoreLibs/crank'
import 'CoreLibs/timer'


gfx=playdate.graphics

--***********************************

function fortune()
gfx.clear()
gfx.setColor(gfx.kColorBlack)
gfx.fillCircleAtPoint(200,120,100)
gfx.setColor(gfx.kColorWhite)
gfx.fillRect(125,105,150,20)
gfx.setColor(gfx.kColorBlack)
```

```lua
    j=math.random(5)

    if j==1 then
      gfx.drawText('definitely yes',160,105)
    end
    if j==2 then
      gfx.drawText('definitely no ',160,105)
    end
    if j==3 then
      gfx.drawText('    maybe     ',160,105)
    end
    if j==4 then
      gfx.drawText('  try again   ',160,105)
    end
    if j==5 then
      gfx.drawText('  be careful  ',160,105)
    end
end

fortune()

--************************************

function playdate.AButtonDown()
  fortune()
end

--************************************

function playdate.update()

  local crankTicks = playdate.getCrankTicks(6)

  if crankTicks~=0 then
    fortune()
  end

end
```

Program 6 - Analog clock

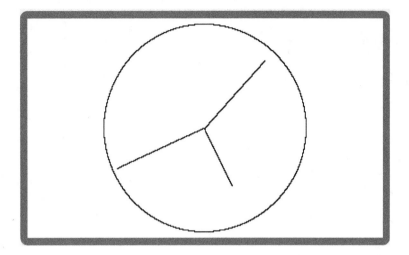

To draw the hands of an analog clock, we must use the following 3 equations:

The second hand and minute hand are the simplest.

We simply take the number of seconds and multiply by 6 to get the number of degrees:

second angle = seconds x 6

We must convert to radians instead of degrees by multiplying by pi divided by 180. Since we are starting from the 12 o'clock position for 0 seconds, we use the sine function to help determine our x coordinate, and the cosine function to help determine the y coordinate.

For minutes,

minute angle = minutes x 6

The most difficult is the hour hand. Since there are 12 hours, each hour is 30 degrees, since 360 / 12 = 30. For each minute that passes by, we must slightly move the hour hand, or else the hour hand will not be in correct position. Since there are 60 minutes in an hour, and each hour is 30 degrees, each minute is a half a degree (30 / 60 = 0.5).

hour angle = (hour x 30) + (minute / 2)

The time can be set by turning the crank counterclockwise to set the minutes and clockwise to set the hours.

When using functions related to time, it is necessary to:

import 'Corelibs/timer'

We must call the function **playdate.timer.performAfterDelay(1000,times)** so that the time is updated every second (1000 milliseconds). The **playdate.timer.performAfterDelay()** function calls the function times() after 1000 milliseconds. Within the **times()** function, we must call **playdate.timer.performAfterDelay()** again to restart the timer. Also, in **playdate.update()** we must call **playdate.timer.updateTimers()**

The download file name is **clock.zip** at my download link.

```
--analog clock
--copyright 2024 R. Tanikawa


import 'CoreLibs/sprites.lua'
import 'CoreLibs/graphics.lua'
import 'CoreLibs/crank'
import 'CoreLibs/timer'


gfx = playdate.graphics


hrs=5
mins=7
tix=30


--***********************************

function times()
  gfx.clear()
  gfx.drawCircleAtPoint(200,120,114)
  gfx.drawLine(200,120,200+(108*math.sin(tix*6*math.pi/180)),120-
(108*math.cos(tix*6*math.pi/180)))
  gfx.drawLine(200,120,200+(100*math.sin(mins*6*math.pi/180)),120-
(100*math.cos(mins*6*math.pi/180)))

gfx.drawLine(200,120,200+(70*math.sin(((hrs*30)+(mins/2))*math.pi/180)
```

```lua
            ),120-(70*math.cos(((hrs*30)+(mins/2))*math.pi/180)))


    tix+=1
    if tix==60 then
      tix=0
      mins+=1
      if mins==60 then
        mins=0
        hrs+=1
        if hrs==13 then
          hrs=1
        end
      end
    end
  end

  playdate.timer.performAfterDelay(1000,times)
end

times()

--***********************************

function playdate.update()

  local crankTicks = playdate.getCrankTicks(6)

  if crankTicks<0 then
    mins=mins-crankTicks
    mins=mins % 60
  end
  if crankTicks>=0 then
    hrs+=crankTicks
    hrs=hrs % 12
  end

  playdate.timer.updateTimers()

end
```

Program 7 - Tic Tac Toe game.

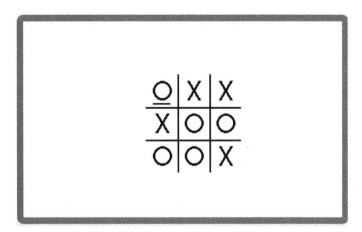

Our first game is Tic Tac Toe. This is a 2 player game. The programming for the computer to move would be much more extensive.

When the crank is turned, it calls the moves1(cval) function with input cval which is the crank value (the function is shown below). The variable pm keeps track of which box (from 1 to 9) we are on. The boxes go across and then down.

1	2	3
4	5	6
7	8	9

We calculate the ax and ay values with these equations:

ax=(pm-1) % 3
ay=math.floor((pm-1)/3)

If you go through the values from 1 to 9 it results in the following:

pm	ax	ay
1	0	0
2	1	0
3	2	0
4	0	1
5	1	1
6	2	1
7	0	2
8	1	2
9	2	2

We then clear the old box selection indicator (we first set gfx.setColor(gx.kColorWhite)). We increase (or decrease) the pm variable by cval with pm+=cval (this means pm=pm+cval)

We then check if pm<1 or pm>9 (I put it on one line of code, but you can split it into 3 lines if you prefer.

Again, we calculate the ax and ay values and draw the new box selection indicator. The variables px and py keep track of which row and column we are on.

```
function moves1(cval)
  ax=(pm-1) % 3
  ay=math.floor((pm-1)/3)
  gfx.setColor(gfx.kColorWhite)
  gfx.drawRect(162+40*ax,100+40*ay,22,2)
  pm+=cval
  if pm<1 then pm=1 end
  if pm>9 then pm=9 end
  ax=(pm-1) % 3
  ay=math.floor((pm-1)/3)
  gfx.setColor(gfx.kColorBlack)
  gfx.drawRect(162+40*ax,100+40*ay,22,2)
```

```
    px=ax
    py=ay
  end
```

When the A button is pressed, we call playdate.AButtonDown(). We set the color to black. First we check if the current box is free (value of 0). We find the correct array element with py*3+px+1. If it is clear, we set it to 1 and then check the color (clr). Really, it is a letter, but I use clr, with 0 being O and 1 being X. Finally we set the new color with that handy mod (%) function: clr=(clr+1) % 2

```
function playdate.AButtonDown()
  gfx.setColor(gfx.kColorBlack)
  if ar[py*3+px+1]==0 then
    ar[py*3+px+1]=1
    if clr==0 then
      gfx.drawText("O",162+40*px,70+40*py)
    else
      gfx.drawText("X",165+40*px,70+40*py)
    end
    clr=(clr+1) % 2
  end
end
```

The download file name is **tictactoe.zip** at my download link.

There is some code for the B button to restart the game. Here is the full program:

```
--tic tac toe
--copyright 2024 R. Tanikawa

import 'CoreLibs/sprites.lua'
import 'CoreLibs/graphics.lua'
import 'CoreLibs/crank'
import 'CoreLibs/timer'

gfx=playdate.graphics

myfonts = gfx.font.new('SystemAssets/Roobert-24-Medium')
gfx.setFont(myfonts)
```

```
px=1
py=1

ar={0,0,0, 0,0,0, 0,0,0}

clr=0
pm=5

--***********************************

function init()
  gfx.clear()
  gfx.setColor(gfx.kColorBlack)
  gfx.drawRect(193,65,2,120)
  gfx.drawRect(233,65,2,120)
  gfx.drawRect(153,105,120,2)
  gfx.drawRect(153,145,120,2)
  pm=5
  clr=0
  for j=1,9,1 do
    ar[j]=0
  end
  moves1(0)
end

--***********************************

function moves1(cval)
  ax=(pm-1) % 3
  ay=math.floor((pm-1)/3)
  gfx.setColor(gfx.kColorWhite)
  gfx.drawRect(162+40*ax,100+40*ay,22,2)
  pm+=cval
  if pm<1 then pm=1 end
  if pm>9 then pm=9 end
  ax=(pm-1) % 3
  ay=math.floor((pm-1)/3)
  gfx.setColor(gfx.kColorBlack)
  gfx.drawRect(162+40*ax,100+40*ay,22,2)
  px=ax
```

```lua
      py=ay
   end

init()


--************************************

function playdate.AButtonDown()
   gfx.setColor(gfx.kColorBlack)
   if ar[py*3+px+1]==0 then
      ar[py*3+px+1]=1
      if clr==0 then
         gfx.drawText("O",162+40*px,70+40*py)
      else
         gfx.drawText("X",165+40*px,70+40*py)
      end
      clr=(clr+1) % 2
   end
end


--************************************

function playdate.BButtonDown()
   gfx.clear()
   init()
   moves1(0)
end

--************************************

function playdate.update()

   local crankTicks = playdate.getCrankTicks(6)

   if crankTicks~=0 then
      moves1(crankTicks)
   end
end
```

Program 8 - 4 in a row

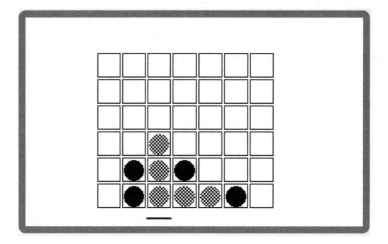

In this 2 player game we turn the crank in function playdate.update() to select the column bx that we want to drop a disc in.

We then call moves(). First we erase the old column selector. Then we ensure the selector is between 0 and 6. Finally we draw the new column selector.

```
function moves()

  gfx.setColor(gfx.kColorWhite)
  gfx.fillRect(85+30*px,230,30,2)

  if bx<0 then
    bx=0
  end

  if bx>6 then
    bx=6
  end

  gfx.setColor(gfx.kColorBlack)
  gfx.fillRect(85+30*bx,230,30,2)
  px=bx
end
```

When the A button is pressed, we first check if the height ht<6. If the color clr is 0 we

have a checkerbox pattern. This is defined using base 16 numbers (hexadecimal).
Please note that a 0 means the pixel is black and 1 menas the pixel is white.

Here is a basic hexadecimal table:

Hex Number	8's	4's	2's	1's
0	0	0	0	0
1	0	0	0	1
2	0	0	1	0
3	0	0	1	1
4	0	1	0	0
5	0	1	0	1
6	0	1	1	0
7	0	1	1	1
8	1	0	0	0
9	1	0	0	1
A	1	0	1	0
B	1	0	1	1
C	1	1	0	0
D	1	1	0	1
E	1	1	1	0
F	1	1	1	1

Here is what gfx.setPattern({ 0xcc, 0xcc, 0x33, 0x33, 0xcc, 0xcc, 0x33, 0x33 }) looks like:

1	1	0	0	1	1	0	0
1	1	0	0	1	1	0	0
0	0	1	1	0	0	1	1
0	0	1	1	0	0	1	1
1	1	0	0	1	1	0	0
1	1	0	0	1	1	0	0
0	0	1	1	0	0	1	1
0	0	1	1	0	0	1	1

For each set of 4 columns, we add the base 2 place value. So 1100 is 8+4 which is the hexadecimal value of C.

8	4	2	1
1	1	0	0

Also 0011 is 0+0+2+1 which is the value of 3. If the color clr is 1 we have a solid black pattern. To draw a filled circle, we use gfx.fillCircleAtPoint(cx,cy,radius) where cx and cy are the x and y location of the center of the circle and radius is the radius.

```
function playdate.AButtonDown()
        if ht[bx+1]<6 then
          if colr==0 then

            gfx.setPattern({ 0xcc, 0xcc, 0x33, 0x33, 0xcc, 0xcc, 0x33,
0x33 })
            gfx.fillCircleAtPoint(100+30*bx,206-30*ht[bx+1],12)

        else
          gfx.setPattern({ 0x00, 0x00, 0x00, 0x00, 0x00, 0x00, 0x00,
0x00 })
            gfx.fillCircleAtPoint(100+30*bx,206-30*ht[bx+1],12)
        end
```

```
            colr=(colr+1) % 2
            ht[bx+1]+=1
        end
end
```

The B button can be pressed to start over.

The download file name is **c4.zip** at my download link.

Here is the entire code:

```lua
--c4 game
--copyright 2024 R. Tanikawa

import 'CoreLibs/sprites.lua'
import 'CoreLibs/graphics.lua'
import 'CoreLibs/crank'
import 'CoreLibs/timer'


gfx=playdate.graphics

n=1

ht={0,0,0,0,0,0,0}
bx=3
px=3
done=0
colr=0

--************************************

function init()
  gfx.clear()
  gfx.setColor(gfx.kColorBlack)

  for i=1,7,1 do
    for j=1,6,1 do
      gfx.drawRect(55+i*30+1,j*30+11,28,28)
```

```
      end
    end

  ht={0,0,0,0,0,0,0}
  bx=3
  px=3
  done=0
  colr=0

  gfx.fillRect(85+30*bx,230,30,2)
end

init()

--*********************************

function moves()

  gfx.setColor(gfx.kColorWhite)
  gfx.fillRect(85+30*px,230,30,2)

  if bx<0 then
    bx=0
  end

  if bx>6 then
    bx=6
  end

  gfx.setColor(gfx.kColorBlack)
  gfx.fillRect(85+30*bx,230,30,2)
  px=bx
end

--*********************************

function playdate.AButtonDown()
      if ht[bx+1]<6 then
        if colr==0 then
```

```
            gfx.setPattern({ 0xcc, 0xcc, 0x33, 0x33, 0xcc, 0xcc, 0x33,
0x33 })
            gfx.fillCircleAtPoint(100+30*bx,206-30*ht[bx+1],12)

        else
            gfx.setPattern({ 0x00, 0x00, 0x00, 0x00, 0x00, 0x00, 0x00,
0x00 })
            gfx.fillCircleAtPoint(100+30*bx,206-30*ht[bx+1],12)
        end

        colr=(colr+1) % 2
        ht[bx+1]+=1
    end
end

--**********************************


function playdate.BButtonDown()
  init()
end

--**********************************


function playdate.update()

  local crankTicks = playdate.getCrankTicks(6)
  playdate.timer.updateTimers()

  if crankTicks~=0 then
    bx=bx+crankTicks
    moves()
  end

end
```

Program 9 - Ball Bounce game

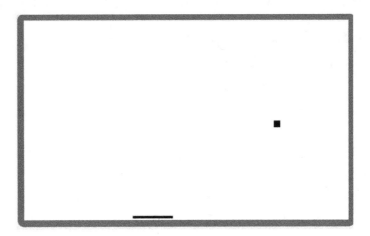

In this game we will introduce the concept of sprites. Sprites are 2D images that are used on the screen and can be moved around. To make a new sprite we call gfx.sprite:new()

Notice that we use a : and not a dot. The Playdate SDC reference says that class/table functions are called with a dot while instance functions are called with a :

Care must be taken to not confuse the two or a bug can result that is difficult to find. For the ball in this ball bounce game, we also set the sprite size and starting location. Finally, we add the sprite.

```
local ball = gfx.sprite:new()
ball:setSize(8,8)
ball:moveTo(200,120)
ball:addSprite()
```

The draw function is simple. We set the color to black and fill an 8x8 rectangle.

```
ball.draw=function()
  gfx.setColor(gfx.kColorBlack)
  gfx.fillRect(0,0,8,8)
end
```

The ball update function is more complicated. To vary the ball motion, we use a variable amp (amplitude) that can randomly range from 1 to 3.

The horizontal direction of the ball bx and vertical direction by can be -1 or 1. The ball location bxx and byy are updated.

We then check if the ball reaches the left or right side of the screen. If it reaches the left side, then bx was -1 and becomes 1. If it reaches the right side, then bx was 1 and becomes -1.

If the ball reaches the top of the screen, then the new direction bx becomes 1 (with by=-by, if the direction was -1, then it changes to 1).

If the ball reaches the bottom of the screen (by>=233), we change the direction by to up. We also set the amplitude amp to a random number from 1 to 3. Finally we check if the ball location is within 25 pixels of the left or right side of the paddle. If it is outside of the paddle, the game ends by setting n to 0. The score is displayed. If the ball hits the paddle, then the score is increased by 1.

Lastly, we call ball:moveTo(bxx,byy)
The paddle draw and update functions are much more straightforward.

```
ball.update=function()
  bxx+=(bx*amp)
  byy+=by
  if (bxx<2) then
     bx=-bx
     bxx=2
  end
  if (bxx>396) then
     bx=-bx
     bxx=396
  end
  if (byy<2) then
    by=-by
    amp=math.random(3)
    byy=2
  end
  if (byy>=233) then
    by=-by
    amp=math.random(3)
    byy=233
    if (bxx<(dx-25)) or (bxx>(dx+25)) then
      n=0
```

```
      else
        score+=1
      end
  end
  ball:moveTo(bxx,byy)
end
```

If you want to remind the user to undock the crank, you can check with `playdate.isCrankDocked()` and call `playdate.ui.crankIndicator:draw()`
Make sure you also have the following line at the beginning of your program:

```
import 'CoreLibs/ui.lua'
```

The playdate.update() function checks if the paddle location dx is within the screen boundaries. If the game mode n is 1 (playing) then we must call gfx.sprite.update(), otherwise, the score is displayed. The A button can be pressed to restart.

```
function playdate.update()

  if playdate.isCrankDocked()==true then
    playdate.ui.crankIndicator:draw()
    return
  end

  local crankTicks = playdate.getCrankTicks(300)

  if crankTicks~=0 then
    dx=dx+crankTicks
    if dx<25 then dx=25 end
    if dx>375 then dx=375 end
  end
  if n==1 then
    gfx.sprite.update()
  else
    gfx.drawText("Score "..score..".  Press A to restart.",90,120)
  end
end
```

The download file name is **bbounce.zip** at my download link.

Here is the entire code:

```
--ball bounce
--copyright 2024 R. Tanikawa
import 'CoreLibs/sprites.lua'
import 'CoreLibs/graphics.lua'
import 'CoreLibs/crank'
import 'CoreLibs/timer'
import 'CoreLibs/ui.lua'

gfx=playdate.graphics

myfonts = gfx.font.new('SystemAssets/Roobert-11-Medium')
gfx.setFont(myfonts)

dx=160
n=1
bx=1
by=3
amp=3
bxx=160
byy=20
score=0

local ball = gfx.sprite:new()
ball:setSize(8,8)
ball:moveTo(200,120)
ball:addSprite()

local paddle = gfx.sprite:new()
paddle:setSize(50,3)
paddle:moveTo(dx,237)
paddle:addSprite()


--**********************************

ball.draw=function()
  gfx.setColor(gfx.kColorBlack)
  gfx.fillRect(0,0,8,8)
end

--**********************************
```

```
paddle.draw=function()
  gfx.setColor(gfx.kColorBlack)
  gfx.fillRect(0,0,50,3)
end

--**********************************

ball.update=function()
  bxx+=(bx*amp)
  byy+=by
  if (bxx<2) then
    bx=-bx
    bxx=2
  end
  if (bxx>396) then
    bx=-bx
    bxx=396
  end
  if (byy<2) then
    by=-by
    amp=math.random(3)
    byy=2
  end
  if (byy>=233) then
    by=-by
    amp=math.random(3)
    byy=233
    if (bxx<(dx-25)) or (bxx>(dx+25)) then
      n=0
    else
      score+=1
    end
  end
  ball:moveTo(bxx,byy)

end

--**********************************

paddle.update=function()
  paddle:moveTo(dx,237)
end

--**********************************
```

```lua
function playdate.AButtonDown()
  n=1
  gfx.setColor(gfx.kColorWhite)
  gfx.fillRect(90,120,180,20)
  gfx.setColor(gfx.kColorBlack)
  score=0
end

--************************************

function playdate.update()

  if playdate.isCrankDocked()==true then
    playdate.ui.crankIndicator:draw()
    return
  end

  local crankTicks = playdate.getCrankTicks(300)

  if crankTicks~=0 then
    dx=dx+crankTicks
    if dx<25 then dx=25 end
    if dx>375 then dx=375 end
  end
  if n==1 then
    gfx.sprite.update()
  else
    gfx.drawText("Score "..score..".  Press A to restart.",90,120)
  end
end
```

Program 10 - Breaker game

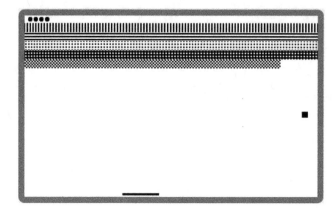

This game is very similar to the Ball Bounce game, but adds the element of bricks that must be removed. To draw the bricks, we use the function reinit()

We have 5 rows of bricks. Below is code for one of the rows. After setting the pattern, we have a for loop that checks if the block is still active (0=empty, 1=active). If the block is active, we draw it. The blocks have to be redrawn because they are not sprites. When gfx.sprite.update() is called, it erases elements of the screen that are not sprites.

```
gfx.setPattern({ 0x66, 0x66, 0x66, 0x66, 0x66, 0x66, 0x66, 0x66 })
for m=1,8,1 do
  if (ar[m]==1) then
    gfx.fillRect((m-1)*50,10,50,12)
  end
end
```

Inside the ball.update function, we have code to check if a brick is encountered. To find the brick number m, we use the following equation:

m=math.floor((byy-14)/12)*8+math.floor(bxx/50)+1

The blocks are offset by 14 pixels, so we do the ball y location byy-14 and then divide by 12 since the blocks are 12 pixels high. We multiply by 8 since each row has 8 blocks. Finally, to find the column, we do the math.floor(bxx/50) function. We take the ball x location bxx and divide by 50. math.floor() is necessary to have an integer number.

If the block is present, we play a sound, set the block to empty (0) and increment the score. If we hit all 40 blocks, we are done. The ball horizontal direction bx and vertical direction by are reversed, and we set amp (amplitude) to a random number from 1 to 3.

```
if (byy<74) then
    m=math.floor((byy-14)/12)*8+math.floor(bxx/50)+1
    if ar[m]==1 then
      s:playNote(110)
      s:noteOff()
      ar[m]=0
      score+=1
      if score==40 then
        n=0
        gfx.setColor(gfx.kColorBlack)
        gfx.drawText("Score "..score..".  Press A to
restart.",90,120)
      end
      bx=-bx
      by=-by
      amp=math.random(3)
    end
end
```

To display the number of lives uses 6 lines of code within the function dolives()

We erase the old number of lives and use a for loop with variable j to draw the current number of lives available by using **gfx.fillCircleAtPoint(j*8,5,3)**

```
function dolives()
  gfx.setColor(gfx.kColorWhite)
  gfx.fillRect(0,0,50,10)
  gfx.setColor(gfx.kColorBlack)
  for j=1,lives,1 do
    gfx.fillCircleAtPoint(j*8,5,3)
  end
end
```

The A button is pressed to restart.

The download file name is **breaker.zip** at my download link.

Here is the code:

```lua
--Breaker game
--copyright 2024 R. Tanikawa

import 'CoreLibs/sprites.lua'
import 'CoreLibs/graphics.lua'
import 'CoreLibs/crank'
import 'CoreLibs/timer'


gfx=playdate.graphics

dx=160
n=1
bx=1
by=3
amp=3
bxx=160
byy=100
score=0
lives=5

ar={}

local snd = playdate.sound

s = snd.synth.new(snd.kWaveTriangle)
s:setDecay(0.5)
s:setSustain(0.6)
s:setRelease(0.5)

local ball = gfx.sprite:new()
ball:setSize(8,8)
ball:moveTo(200,120)
ball:addSprite()
```

```lua
local paddle = gfx.sprite:new()
paddle:setSize(50,3)
paddle:moveTo(dx,237)
paddle:addSprite()

ball.draw=function()
  gfx.setColor(gfx.kColorBlack)
  gfx.fillRect(0,0,8,8)
end

paddle.draw=function()
  gfx.setColor(gfx.kColorBlack)
  gfx.fillRect(0,0,50,3)
end

paddle.update=function()
  paddle:moveTo(dx,237)
end

  --**********************************
function reinit()
  gfx.setPattern({ 0x66, 0x66, 0x66, 0x66, 0x66, 0x66, 0x66, 0x66 })
  for m=1,8,1 do
    if (ar[m]==1) then
      gfx.fillRect((m-1)*50,10,50,12)
    end
  end

  gfx.setPattern({ 0x00, 0xff, 0xff, 0x00, 0x00, 0xff, 0xff, 0x00 })
  for m=9,16,1 do
    if (ar[m]==1) then
      gfx.fillRect((m-9)*50,22,50,12)
    end
  end

  gfx.setPattern({ 0xff, 0x99, 0x99, 0xff, 0xff, 0x99, 0x99, 0xff })
  for m=17,24,1 do
    if (ar[m]==1) then
      gfx.fillRect((m-17)*50,34,50,12)
```

```
      end
    end

    gfx.setPattern({ 0x00, 0x66, 0x66, 0x00, 0x00, 0x66, 0x66, 0x00 })
    for m=25,32,1 do
      if (ar[m]==1) then
        gfx.fillRect((m-25)*50,46,50,12)
      end
    end

    gfx.setPattern({ 0xcc, 0xcc, 0x33, 0x33, 0xcc, 0xcc, 0x33, 0x33 })
    for m=33,40,1 do
      if (ar[m]==1) then
        gfx.fillRect((m-33)*50,58,50,12)
      end
    end
end

for k=1,40,1
do
  ar[k]=1
end

reinit()

  --***********************************
function dolives()
  gfx.setColor(gfx.kColorWhite)
  gfx.fillRect(0,0,50,10)
  gfx.setColor(gfx.kColorBlack)
  for j=1,lives,1 do
    gfx.fillCircleAtPoint(j*8,5,3)
  end
end

dolives()

  --***********************************
ball.update=function()
```

```lua
    bxx+=(bx*amp)
    byy+=by
    if (bxx<1) then
       bx=-bx
       bxx=0
    end
    if (bxx>396) then
       bx=-bx
       bxx=396
    end
    if (byy<10) then
       by=-by
       amp=math.random(3)
       byy=10
    end

    if (byy<74) then
       m=math.floor((byy-14)/12)*8+math.floor(bxx/50)+1
       if ar[m]==1 then
          s:playNote(110)
          s:noteOff()
          ar[m]=0
          score+=1
          if score==40 then
             n=0
             gfx.setColor(gfx.kColorBlack)
             gfx.drawText("Score "..score..".  Press A to
restart.",90,120)
          end
          bx=-bx
          by=-by
          amp=math.random(3)
       end
    end

    if (byy>=233) then
       by=-by
       amp=math.random(3)
       byy=233
```

```lua
      if (bxx<(dx-25)) or (bxx>(dx+25)) then
        lives-=1
        dolives()
        if lives==0 then
          n=0
         gfx.setColor(gfx.kColorBlack)
          gfx.drawText("Score "..score..".  Press A to
restart.",90,120)
        end
      else
        s:playNote(110)
        s:noteOff()
      end
    end
    ball:moveTo(bxx,byy)
end


  --*********************************
function playdate.AButtonDown()
  n=1
  gfx.setColor(gfx.kColorWhite)
  gfx.fillRect(90,120,180,20)
  gfx.setColor(gfx.kColorBlack)
  score=0
  lives=5
  for k=1,40,1
  do
    ar[k]=1
  end
  reinit()
  dolives()
end


  --***********************************
function playdate.update()

  local crankTicks = playdate.getCrankTicks(200)

  if crankTicks~=0 then
```

```lua
      dx=dx+crankTicks
      if dx<25 then dx=25 end
      if dx>375 then dx=375 end
   end
   if n==1 then
      gfx.sprite.update()
   else
      gfx.setColor(gfx.kColorBlack)
      gfx.drawText("Score "..score..".  Press A to restart.",90,120)
   end
   reinit()
   dolives()

end
```

Program 11 - Animation example.

To do animation, you will need to use an image table. Below is an example of one:

You would a paint program (like Windows Paint) to do the drawing. I actually drew one of the images, and then used the rotate function in Windows Paint to make the other 3.

An application called Tiled is extremely useful in producing animation and tilemaps (used in programs 12 and 13). Tiled can be found at: http://www.mapeditor.org/

You will have to download the program and then install it.

The smiley faces are 32x32 pixels. In Windows Paint, you can specify the image size by pixels. To actually edit the image, you need to zoom in to it.

First, in Tiled, select File->New->New Project. Give your project a name and then select New Tileset. Give your tileset a name, select Collection of Images … and click on Save As. Click on the + symbol to add images to your tileset and then save it.

But we're not done yet. Now select File->New->New Map. The map size will be a fixed size of width 4 tiles and height 1 tile. The tile size will be 32 pixels wide and 32 pixels in height. Now you will insert the 4 smiley faces into your tilemap. Save your tilemap.

One final step is that we go to File->Export as Image to export the tilemap as a .PNG file, like smiley.png. This file has to be renamed to a Playdate format that ends in - table-32-32

The new name would be smiley-table-32-32.png

This file has to be placed in the SystemAssets subdirectory of your Playdate program. Make sure you import 'CoreLibs/animation.lua'

The first thing to do is call gfx.imagetable.new(). You can give the subdirectory name and just smiley.

```
local animationImagetable = gfx.imagetable.new("SystemAssets/smiley")
```
Then we call gfx.animation.loop.new(frameTime,animationImagetable,true)

The last argument is if the animation should loop, or not.

In playdate.update(), a call to animationLoop:draw(x,y) must be called. The program below causes the smiley face to animate and bounce back and forth across the screen.

The download file name is **smiley.zip** at my download link.

```
--Smiley animation
--copyright 2024 R. Tanikawa

import 'CoreLibs/animation.lua'

local gfx = playdate.graphics

dx=3
gx=184

local frameTime = 800
local animationImagetable = gfx.imagetable.new("SystemAssets/smiley")

local animationLoop = gfx.animation.loop.new(frameTime,
animationImagetable, true)

--**********************************
function playdate.update()

    gfx.clear()
    animationLoop:draw(gx, 104)
   gx+=dx
   if gx>368 then
     gx=368
     dx=-dx
   else
     if gx<1 then
       gx=1
       dx=-dx
     end
   end
end
```

Program 12 - Pizza Maze

This is an eat the pellets and avoid the monster maze type game. Games using tilemaps are considered more advanced to make and will require extra effort to make, debug and understand. The basics of making images and using Tiled to make a .PNG file are similar to the last animation example.

Here is my imagetable picture, pizza-table-16-16.png

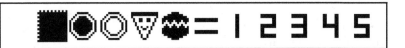

It's not easy to see it, but there's a blank square before the black square.
But then we make another tilemap of the actual game, like below:

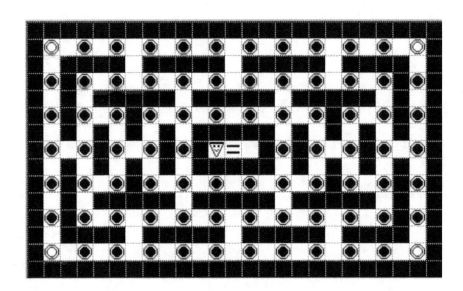

The size of each tile is 16x16 pixels, and the Tilemap is 25x15 tiles (which fits on the Playdate screen). Once you have made your tilemap, you have to export it, by selecting File->Export As …

In the dialog box, select the type as CSV files. CSV means comma separated values. You will then have to open the .CSV file and copy the text and paste it into your Playdate program, adding a { at the beginning, commas at the end of each row and a } at the end. I call my tilemap aa, so:

aa={2,2,2,2, … }

You will need to initialize the image table and then setup your tilemap.

```
function init()
    spritesheet = gfx.imagetable.new("SystemAssets/pizza-table-16-16")
    tilemap = gfx.tilemap.new()
    tilemap:setImageTable(spritesheet)
end
```

After calling the init() function, it is important to call setTiles to tell the Playdate which table to use and the width of the tilemap: tilemap:setTiles(aa, 25)

One of the key functions for converting the player's x and y coordinates on the screen into the aa table index is below. The table size is 25x15 or a size of 375.

The first part math.floor((ay-1)/16)+1)*25 finds the correct "row" of 25 in table aa. The second part math.floor((ax-1)/16)+2 finds the correct "column". We add 2 because we subtracted 1 and because Lua accesses tables starting with an index of 1. Finally, the type of object at that position is returned, based on the original pizza-table-16-16.png image table (1=blank, 2=wall, 3=regular pellet, 4=special pellet, 5=pizza, etc.)

```
--  ******************************************************
function checkit(ax,ay)
  arrayidx=(math.floor((ay-1)/16)+1)*25+math.floor((ax-1)/16)+2
  return aa[arrayidx]
end
```

The Playdate buttonDown functions set the correct x and y change values. We use 2's so the player can move faster than the enemies.

```
function playdate.leftButtonDown()
  dx=-2
  dy=0
end
```

We also have buttonUp functions to set the x and y change values to 0.

```
function playdate.leftButtonUp()
  dx=0
end
```

In the enemymove() function, we compare the player's coordinates to the enemy's and adjust the enemy's position accordingly. For ex and ey we have 2, so we use the table notation ex[k], where k is a for loop counter from 1 to 2.

```
if px<ex[k] then
   ex[k]-=0.25
 end
```

We also have to check if the player collided with the enemy

```
if math.abs(ex[1]-px)<8 and math.abs(ey[1]-py)<8 then
```

If this happens, we lose a life, check if the game is over, play a sound, update the lives display on the screen, and reset the enemy's position. Since we changed the number of lives (displayed in the middle of the screen), we have to call tilemap:setTiles(aa,25)

```
   lives-=1
   if lives==0 then
      gamend()
   end

   s:playNote(110)
   s:noteOff()

   aa[189]=7+lives
   ex[1]=16
   ey[1]=112
   tilemap:setTiles(aa, 25)
```

In pizzaction(), we check if check if there is a pellet (3) or a special pellet (4).

If so, make that square blank (aa[arrayidx]=1), increase the score and see if all pellets have been eaten (to end the game). Also play a sound, and call `tilemap:setTiles(aa, 25)`, Unlike the popular game, when you eat a special pellet, the monsters go back to their starting place, so if the piece is 4, reset both monsters ex and ey coordinates.

```
function pizzaction()
  piece=checkit(px,py)

  if piece==3 or piece==4 then
    arrayidx=(math.floor((py-1)/16)+1)*25+math.floor((px-1)/16)+2
    aa[arrayidx]=1
```

```
      score+=1
      if score==82 then
         gamend()
      end

      s:playNote(440)
      s:noteOff()

      tilemap:setTiles(aa, 25)
      if piece==4 then
         ex={16,368}
         ey={112,112}
      end
   end
end
```

The pizzamove() function is one of the longer and more difficult functions to implement. It can be shorter if we didn't check for the pizza character being close to a opening when changing directions.

For example, if you are moving left, and want to move up (or down) through an opening in the maze, we make the pizza character jump to the location where the maze opening is. The first thing to do is call checkit(). If moving left, we give px-16 for the x coordinate to check if there is a wall to the left. The code that compares diff to mlow and mhigh sees if the pizza character is close enough to a wall opening.

If there is a wall (no opening), dx is set to 0, so the player stops moving.

```
  mlow=6
  mhigh=10

 if dx==-2 then

    if checkit(px-16,py-8)~=2 then
      diff=py % 16
      if diff<mlow then
         py-=diff
         px-=2
      else
         if diff>mhigh then
            py+=(16-diff)
            px-=2
         end
      end
    else
      dx=0
```

```
        end
    end
```

In gamend(), we set gamestate to 0 to stop the game and display a message to press the A button to restart.

So the playdate.AButtonDown() function resets variables, reinitializes the level and calls tilemap:setTiles(aa, 25)

playdate.update() has to move the pizza, move the enemies, draw the tilemap, and draw the pizza and enemies (we must draw the pizza and enemies after drawing the tilemap, because the tilemap will erase anything drawn before it).

```
pizzamove()
enemymove()
tilemap:draw(0,0)
pizzaimg:draw(px,py)
enemyimg:draw(ex[1],ey[1])
enemyimg1:draw(ex[2],ey[2])
```

The download file name is **pizza.zip** at my download link.

```
--pizza maze game
--copyright 2024 R. Tanikawa

import 'CoreLibs/sprites.lua'
import 'CoreLibs/graphics.lua'
import 'CoreLibs/crank'
import 'CoreLibs/timer'

-- ***********************************************
function initlevel()
aa={2,2,2,2,2,2,2,2,2,2,2,2,2,2,2,2,2,2,2,2,2,2,2,2,2,
2,4,1,3,1,3,1,3,1,3,1,3,1,3,1,3,1,3,1,3,1,3,1,4,2,
2,1,2,2,2,2,1,2,2,2,2,2,1,2,2,2,2,2,1,2,2,2,2,1,2,
2,3,2,3,1,3,1,3,1,3,1,3,1,3,1,3,1,3,1,3,1,3,2,3,2,
2,1,2,1,2,2,2,2,2,1,2,2,2,2,2,1,2,2,2,2,2,1,2,1,2,
2,3,2,3,1,3,2,3,1,3,1,3,1,3,1,3,1,3,2,3,1,3,2,3,2,
2,1,2,1,2,1,2,1,2,1,2,2,2,2,2,1,2,1,2,1,2,1,2,1,2,
2,3,1,3,2,3,1,3,2,3,2,5,7,12,2,3,2,3,1,3,2,3,1,3,2,
```

```
2,1,2,1,2,1,2,1,2,1,2,2,2,2,2,1,2,1,2,1,2,1,2,1,2,
2,3,2,3,1,3,2,3,1,3,1,3,1,3,1,3,1,3,2,3,1,3,2,3,2,
2,1,2,1,2,2,2,2,2,1,2,2,2,2,2,1,2,2,2,2,2,1,2,1,2,
2,3,2,3,1,3,1,3,1,3,1,3,1,3,1,3,1,3,1,3,1,3,2,3,2,
2,1,2,2,2,2,1,2,2,2,2,2,1,2,2,2,2,2,1,2,2,2,2,1,2,
2,4,1,3,1,3,1,3,1,3,1,3,1,3,1,3,1,3,1,3,1,3,1,4,2,
2,2,2,2,2,2,2,2,2,2,2,2,2,2,2,2,2,2,2,2,2,2,2,2,2}
end


initlevel()


px=192
py=144
gamestate=1
gfx=playdate.graphics
local snd = playdate.sound


class('MySprite').extends(playdate.graphics.sprite)


local pizzaimg = gfx.image.new('SystemAssets/pizza')
local enemyimg = gfx.image.new('SystemAssets/mouth')
local enemyimg1 = gfx.image.new('SystemAssets/mouth')


s = snd.synth.new(snd.kWaveTriangle)
s:setDecay(0.5)
s:setSustain(0.6)
s:setRelease(0.5)


ex={16,368}
ey={112,112}
score=0
lives=5


local spritesheet = nil -- this will be the image table
local map = nil -- this is the tile map

-- *********************************************
function init() -- needs to be called before update
    spritesheet = gfx.imagetable.new("SystemAssets/pizza-table-16-16")
    tilemap = gfx.tilemap.new()
```

```
    tilemap:setImageTable(spritesheet)
--     tilemap:setSize(10,4)
end


init()


tilemap:setTiles(aa, 25)


-- ***********************************************
function checkit(ax,ay)
  arrayidx=(math.floor((ay-1)/16)+1)*25+math.floor((ax-1)/16)+2
  return aa[arrayidx]
end


-- ***********************************************
function playdate.leftButtonDown()
  dx=-2
  dy=0
end


-- ***********************************************
function playdate.rightButtonDown()
  dx=2
  dy=0
end


-- ***********************************************
function playdate.upButtonDown()
  dy=-2
  dx=0
end


-- ***********************************************
function playdate.downButtonDown()
  dy=2
  dx=0
end


-- ***********************************************
function playdate.leftButtonUp()
```

```lua
    dx=0
  end


-- ************************************************
function playdate.rightButtonUp()
  dx=0
end


-- ************************************************
function playdate.upButtonUp()
  dy=0
end


-- ************************************************
function playdate.downButtonUp()
  dy=0
end


-- ************************************************
function enemymove()
  for k=1,2,1 do
  if px<ex[k] then
    ex[k]-=0.25
  end

  if px>ex[k] then
    ex[k]+=0.25
  end

  if py<ey[k] then
    ey[k]-=0.25
  end

  if py>ey[k] then
      ey[k]+=0.25
  end

  if math.abs(ex[1]-px)<8 and math.abs(ey[1]-py)<8 then
    lives-=1
    if lives==0 then
```

```
        gamend()
      end


      s:playNote(110)
      s:noteOff()

      aa[189]=7+lives
      ex[1]=16
      ey[1]=112
      tilemap:setTiles(aa, 25)
    else
      if math.abs(ex[2]-px)<8 and math.abs(ey[2]-py)<8 then
        lives-=1
        if lives==0 then
          gamend()
        end

        s:playNote(110)
        s:noteOff()
        aa[189]=7+lives
        ex[2]=168
        ey[2]=112
        tilemap:setTiles(aa, 25)
      end
    end
  end
end


-- ***********************************************
function pizzaction()
  piece=checkit(px,py)

  if piece==3 or piece==4 then
    arrayidx=(math.floor((py-1)/16)+1)*25+math.floor((px-1)/16)+2
    aa[arrayidx]=1
    score+=1
    if score==82 then
      gamend()
    end
```

```
    s:playNote(440)
    s:noteOff()

    tilemap:setTiles(aa, 25)
    if piece==4 then
      ex={16,368}
      ey={112,112}
    end

  end
end

-- ***********************************************
function pizzamove()

  mlow=6
  mhigh=10

  if dx==-2 then

    if checkit(px-16,py-8)~=2 then
      diff=py % 16
      if diff<mlow then
        py-=diff
        px-=2
      else
        if diff>mhigh then
          py+=(16-diff)
      px-=2
        end
      end
    else
      dx=0
    end
  end

  if dx==2 then
    if checkit(px+1,py-8)~=2 then
      diff=py % 16
      if diff<mlow then
```

```lua
        py-=diff
        px+=2
      else if diff>mhigh then
        py+=(16-diff)
      px+=2
        end
      end
    else
      dx=0
    end
  end

  if dy==-2 then
    if checkit(px-8,py-16)~=2 then
      diff=px % 16
      if diff<mlow then
        px-=diff
        py-=2
      else if diff>mhigh then
        px+=(16-diff)
      py-=2
        end
      end
    else
      dy=0
    end
  end

  if dy==2 then
    if checkit(px-8,py+1)~=2 then
      diff=px % 16
      if diff<mlow then
        px-=diff
        py+=2
      else if diff>mhigh then
        px+=(16-diff)
      py+=2
        end
      end
    else
```

```lua
      dy=0
    end
  end

  if px<16 then px=16 end
  if px>368 then px=368 end
  if py<16 then py=16 end
  if py>208 then py=208 end
  pizzaction()
end


-- ************************************************
function gamend()
  gamestate=0
  gfx.setColor(gfx.kColorWhite)
  gfx.fillRect(100,40,200,40)
  gfx.setColor(gfx.kColorBlack)
  gfx.clear()

  gfx.drawText("Game Over.  Press A to restart.",100,40)
end

-- ************************************************
function playdate.AButtonDown()
  lives=5
  score=0

  px=192
  py=144

  initlevel()
  gamestate=1
  ex={92,292}
  ey={1,1}
  gfx.clear()
  tilemap:setTiles(aa, 25)

end


-- ************************************************
```

```
function playdate.update()
  if gamestate==0 then
    gamend()
    return
  end
  if playdate.buttonIsPressed(playdate.kButtonUp) or
    playdate.buttonIsPressed(playdate.kButtonDown) or
    playdate.buttonIsPressed(playdate.kButtonLeft) or
    playdate.buttonIsPressed(playdate.kButtonRight) then
    pizzamove()
  end

  enemymove()
  tilemap:draw(0,0)
  pizzaimg:draw(px,py)
  enemyimg:draw(ex[1],ey[1])
  enemyimg1:draw(ex[2],ey[2])
end
```

Program 13 - Treasure Hunt

Treasure Hunt is a side scroller game. There are many similarities to the Pizza Maze game. I will explain the key differences. First, the tilemap is much bigger. It is 126 tiles wide by 11 tiles tall. Here is the tilemap. I did not include the 13 extra spaces on the left and right sides, which allow us to draw the tilemap with the player on the far left or right side of the maze without it being null.

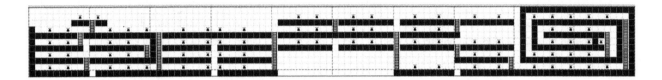

Here is the tilemap for treasure-table-16-16.png. Image 1=wall, 2=gold, 3=ladder and 4=empty space.

The checkit() function is slightly different:

```
function checkit(ax,ay)
  arrayidx=(math.floor((ay-1)/16)-3)*126+math.floor((ax-1)/16)+14
  return aa[arrayidx]
end
```

To calculate the "row" index in our tilemap table aa, we use: `math.floor((ay-1)/16)-3)*126`

Since the Playdate screen starts at coordinates (0,0), we first subtract 1 from ay. We divide by 16 because each tile is 16 pixels tall. We have to subtract 3, because we skip rows 0 to 3 and draw the tilemap on rows 4 to 14. Finally multiply by 126 since each row is 126 tiles wide.

The calculation for the table column is: `math.floor((ax-1)/16)+14`

We subtract 1 from ax for the same reason we did for ay and divide by 16 for the tile width. We add 14 because we skip 13 columns of padding on the left (and right) sides of the maze. An additional 1 is needed because Lua tables start at 1 (13+1=14).

Enemy movement in enemymove() is a little different than Pizza Maze.

ex[1]=gx % 200
ey[1]=(ey[1]+1) % 240

The enemies take the player's x coordinate and use the mod 200 function so that 2 can appear on the screen, equally spaced apart. The enemies move down from the top and when they reach the bottom, they return to the top, so we use (ey[1]+1) % 240.

The personmove() function is similar to pizzamove(). The key difference is when moving up and down, we must check if there's a ladder (3).

if checkit(gx,gy)==3 then …

Also, we check if we have moved to a place where there is empty ground (4) underneath. We must use a for loop to see how far down we fall. Each time, we increase the player's gy coordinate by 16. If there's a solid block (1), we stop falling. If we fall past the bottom (gy>=223), we lose a life, and if lives==0 then the game ends.

```
if checkit(gx-8,gy+1)==4 then
    for r=1,11,1 do
       gy+=16
       if checkit(gx-8,gy+1)==1 or checkit(gx-8,gy+1)==3 then
         break
       end
       if gy>=223 then
         break
       end
    end
  end
if gy>=223 then
    lives-=1
    if lives==0 then
      gamend()
    end
```

The personaction() function checks if the square we're on is gold (2). If so, we replace it with a blank space (4) in the tilemap table aa. We increase the score by 1, and if it's 85 we have reached the end of the game. We play a sound when gold is taken and have to call `tilemap:setTiles(aa, 126)` to set the tilemap to the updated table aa.

```
function personaction()
  piece=checkit(gx,gy)

  if piece==2 then
    arrayidx=(math.floor((gy-1)/16)-3)*126+math.floor((gx-1)/16)+14
    aa[arrayidx]=4
    score+=1
    if score==85 then
      gamend()
    end

    s:playNote(660)
    s:noteOff()

    tilemap:setTiles(aa, 126)
  end
end
```

The key to side scrolling is in the playdate.update() function. The person always stays in the middle of the screen horizontally (but can move up and down vertically).

We call tilemap:draw(0,64,gx,0,399,176) with a position of (0,64). The next 4 parameters are the rectangle (x,y) of (gx,0) which is at the horizontal position gx (in pixels) in the tilemap and 0 (because we're always drawing from the top). If this game scrolled both horizontally and vertically, the 0 would be a variable. (399,176) is the rectangle size, which fills the bottom 176 pixels, starting at 64 (second argument of this function call).

If any of the direction buttons were held down, we call personmove(). We also call enemymove(). The tilemap is then drawn, and we last draw the person and enemies.

```
if playdate.buttonIsPressed(playdate.kButtonUp) or
   playdate.buttonIsPressed(playdate.kButtonDown) or
   playdate.buttonIsPressed(playdate.kButtonLeft) or
   playdate.buttonIsPressed(playdate.kButtonRight) then

  personmove()
end
```

```lua
  enemymove()
  tilemap:draw(0,64,gx,0,399,176)
  personimg:draw(192,gy)
  enemyimg:draw(ex[1],ey[1])
  enemyimg1:draw(ex[2],ey[2])
```

The download file name is **treasure.zip** at my download link.

```lua
--treasure hunt game
--copyright 2024 R. Tanikawa

import 'CoreLibs/sprites.lua'
import 'CoreLibs/graphics.lua'
import 'CoreLibs/crank'
import 'CoreLibs/timer'


-- ***********************************************
function initlevel()
aa={4,4,4,4,4, 4,4,4,4,4,4,4,4,
4,4,4,4,4,4,4,4,4,4,4,4,4,4,4,4,4,4,4,4,4,4,4,4,4,4,4,4,4,4,4,4,
4,4,4,4,4,4,4,4,4,4,4,4,4,4,4,4,4,4,4,4,4,4,4,4,4,4,4,4,4,4,4,4,
4,4,4,4,4,4,4,4,4,4,4,1,1,1,1,1,1,1,1,1,1,1,1,1,1,1,1,1,1,4,4,4,4,4,
4,4,4,4,4,4,4,4,
4,4,4,4,4, 4,4,4,4,4, 4,4,4,
4,4,4,4,4,4,4,4,2,4,4,2,4,4,4,4,4,4,4,4,4,4,4,4,4,4,4,4,4,4,4,4,4,4,
4,4,4,4,4,4,4,4,2,4,4,2,4,4,4,4,2,4,4,2,4,4,4,4,4,2,4,4,2,4,4,
4,4,4,2,4,4,4,2,4,4,4,1,4,2,4,4,2,4,4,2,4,4,2,4,4,2,4,4,4,1,
4,4,4,4,4, 4,4,4,4,4, 4,4,4,
4,4,4,4,4, 4,4,4,4,4, 4,4,4,
4,4,4,4,4,4,4,1,1,1,3,1,1,4,4,4,4,4,4,4,4,4,4,4,4,4,4,4,4,4,4,4,4,4,
4,4,4,4,4,4,1,1,1,1,1,1,1,1,1,1,3,1,1,1,1,1,1,1,1,4,1,1,1,1,1,1,1,1,
3,1,1,1,1,1,1,1,1,1,4,1,4,1,1,1,1,1,1,1,1,1,1,1,1,1,1,3,1,
4,4,4,4,4, 4,4,4,4,4, 4,4,4,
4,4,4,4,4, 4,4,4,4,4, 4,4,4,
1,4,4,2,4,4,2,0,0,0,3,0,0,2,4,4,2,4,4,2,4,4,4,4,4,2,4,4,4,2,4,2,4,4,4,
2,4,4,4,4,4,4,4,4,2,4,4,2,4,4,3,4,4,2,4,4,2,4,4,4,4,4,4,2,4,4,4,2,4,4,
3,4,4,4,4,4,4,4,4,4,1,4,1,4,4,2,4,4,2,0,0,2,4,4,4,4,1,3,1,4,4,4,4,4,
4,4,4,4,4, 4,4,4,
4,4,4,4,4, 4,4,4,4,4, 4,4,4,
1,1,1,1,1,1,1,1,3,1,1,1,1,1,1,1,1,1,1,1,1,1,3,1,1,1,1,1,1,1,1,1,1,1,1,
```

```
1,1,1,1,1,3,1,1,1,1,1,1,1,1,1,1,1,1,1,1,1,1,1,1,1,1,1,3,1,1,1,1,1,1,1,1,1,
1,4,4,4,4,4,4,4,4,4,4,1,4,1,4,1,1,1,1,1,1,1,1,1,1,3,4,1,3,1,4,4,4,4,4,
4,4,4,4,4, 4,4,4,
4,4,4,4,4, 4,4,4,4,4, 4,4,4,
1,4,4,2,4,4,2,4,3,4,4,4,4,2,4,4,2,4,4,4,1,3,4,4,4,2,4,4,4,2,4,2,4,4,4,
2,4,4,4,4,3,4,4,4,2,4,4,2,4,4,4,4,4,2,4,4,2,4,4,4,3,4,4,2,4,4,4,2,4,4,
4,4,4,2,4,4,4,2,4,4,4,1,4,1,4,4,2,4,4,2,4,4,2,1,2,3,4,1,3,1,4,4,4,4,4,
4,4,4,4,4, 4,4,4,
4,4,4,4,4, 4,4,4,4,4, 4,4,4,
1,1,1,1,1,1,1,1,1,4,1,1,1,1,1,1,1,1,1,1,3,1,3,1,1,1,1,1,1,1,1,4,1,1,1,1,
1,1,1,1,1,3,1,1,1,1,1,1,1,1,1,1,4,1,1,1,1,1,1,1,1,1,3,1,1,1,1,1,1,1,1,1,
3,1,1,1,1,1,1,1,1,1,4,1,4,1,1,1,1,1,1,1,1,1,1,1,1,1,3,4,1,3,1,4,4,4,4,4,
4,4,4,4,4, 4,4,4,
4,4,4,4,4, 4,4,4,4,4, 4,4,4,
1,4,4,2,4,4,2,4,4,4,4,4,2,4,4,2,4,4,3,1,3,4,4,4,2,4,4,4,2,4,2,4,4,4,
2,4,4,4,4,3,4,4,4,4,4,4,4,4,4,4,4,4,4,4,4,4,4,4,4,3,4,4,4,4,4,4,4,4,4,
3,4,4,2,4,4,4,2,4,4,4,1,4,2,4,4,2,4,4,2,4,4,2,4,4,3,4,1,3,1,4,4,4,4,4,
4,4,4,4,4, 4,4,4,
4,4,4,4,4, 4,4,4,4,4, 4,4,4,
1,1,1,1,1,1,1,1,1,3,1,3,1,1,1,1,1,1,1,1,1,1,3,1,1,1,1,1,1,1,1,1,4,1,1,1,1,
1,1,1,1,1,3,4,4,4,4,4,4,4,4,4,4,4,4,4,4,4,4,4,4,3,4,4,4,4,4,4,4,4,4,
1,1,1,1,1,1,1,1,1,3,4,1,1,1,1,1,1,1,1,1,1,1,1,1,1,1,1,1,1,3,1,4,4,4,4,4,
4,4,4,4,4, 4,4,4,
4,4,4,4,4, 4,4,4,4,4, 4,4,4,
1,4,4,2,4,4,2,4,4,3,4,3,4,2,4,4,2,4,4,2,4,3,4,4,4,2,4,4,4,2,4,2,4,4,4,
2,4,4,4,4,3,4,4,4,4,4,4,4,4,4,4,4,4,4,4,4,4,4,4,4,4,3,4,4,2,4,4,4,2,4,4,
4,4,4,2,4,4,4,2,4,3,4,4,4,2,4,4,2,4,4,2,4,4,2,4,4,2,4,4,3,1,4,4,4,4,4,
4,4,4,4,4, 4,4,4,
4,4,4,4,4, 4,4,4,4,4, 4,4,4,
1,1,1,1,1,1,1,1,1,1,4,1,1,1,1,1,1,1,1,1,1,1,1,1,1,1,1,1,1,1,4,1,1,1,1,
1,1,1,1,1,1,4,4,4,4,4,4,4,4,4,4,4,4,4,4,4,4,4,4,1,1,1,1,1,1,1,1,1,1,1,
4,1,1,1,1,1,1,1,1,1,1,1,1,1,1,1,1,1,1,1,1,1,1,1,1,1,1,1,1,1,4,4,4,4,4,
4,4,4,4,4, 4,4,4,}
end

px=192
py=144
gx=192
gy=208
```

```
gfx=playdate.graphics

class('MySprite').extends(playdate.graphics.sprite)

local pizzaimg = gfx.image.new('SystemAssets/person')
local enemyimg = gfx.image.new('SystemAssets/mouth')
local enemyimg1 = gfx.image.new('SystemAssets/mouth')

gamestate=1
ex={92,292}
ey={1,1}
score=0
lives=7

initlevel()

local snd = playdate.sound

s = snd.synth.new(snd.kWaveTriangle)
s:setDecay(0.5)
s:setSustain(0.6)
s:setRelease(0.5)

local spritesheet = nil -- this will be the image table
local map = nil -- this is the tile map

--  *********************************************
function init()
    spritesheet = gfx.imagetable.new("SystemAssets/treasurem-table-16-
16")
    tilemap = gfx.tilemap.new()
    tilemap:setImageTable(spritesheet)
    tilemap:setSize(4,1)
end

init()

local myLevel = {}

tilemap:setTiles(aa, 126)
```

```lua
-- ***********************************************
function checkit(ax,ay)
  arrayidx=(math.floor((ay-1)/16)-3)*126+math.floor((ax-1)/16)+14
  return aa[arrayidx]
end

-- ***********************************************
function playdate.leftButtonDown()
  dx=-2
  dy=0
end

-- ***********************************************
function playdate.rightButtonDown()
  dx=2
  dy=0
end

-- ***********************************************
function playdate.upButtonDown()
  dy=-2
  dx=0
end

-- ***********************************************
function playdate.downButtonDown()
  dy=2
  dx=0
end

-- ***********************************************
function playdate.leftButtonUp()
  dx=0
end

-- ***********************************************
function playdate.rightButtonUp()
  dx=0
end
```

```lua
-- ***********************************************
function playdate.upButtonUp()
  dy=0
end

-- ***********************************************
function playdate.downButtonUp()
  dy=0
end

-- ***********************************************
function enemymove()
  gfx.setColor(gfx.kColorWhite)
  gfx.fillRect(ex[1],ey[1],16,16)
  gfx.fillRect(ex[2],ey[2],16,16)
  gfx.setColor(gfx.kColorBlack)


  ex[1]=gx % 200
  ey[1]=(ey[1]+1) % 240

  ex[2]=(gx % 200)+200
  ey[2]=(ey[2]+1) % 240

  if math.abs(ex[1]-px)<8 and math.abs(ey[1]-gy)<8 then
    lives-=1
    if lives==0 then
      gamend()
    end

    s:playNote(110)
    s:noteOff()

    gx-=100

  else
    if math.abs(ex[2]-px)<8 and math.abs(ey[2]-gy)<8 then
      lives-=1
      if lives==0 then gamend() end
```

```lua
        s:playNote(110)
        s:noteOff()
        gx-=100
      end
    end

end

-- **********************************************
function pizzaction()
  piece=checkit(gx,gy)

  if piece==2 then
    arrayidx=(math.floor((gy-1)/16)-3)*126+math.floor((gx-1)/16)+14
    aa[arrayidx]=4
    score+=1
    if score==85 then
      gamend()
    end

    s:playNote(660)
    s:noteOff()

    tilemap:setTiles(aa, 126)
  end
end

-- **********************************************
function resetpizza()
  gx-=120
  if gx<120 then
    gx=120
  end

  gy=208
end

-- **********************************************
function pizzamove()
```

```
mlow=4
mhigh=12

if dx==-2 then

   if checkit(gx-16,gy)~=1 then
     diff=gy % 16
     if diff<mlow then
       gy-=diff
       gx-=2
     else
       if diff>mhigh then
         gy+=(16-diff)
       gx-=2
       end
     end
   else
     dx=0
   end
end

if dx==2 then
   if checkit(gx+1,gy)~=1 then
     diff=gy % 16
     if diff<mlow then
       gy-=diff
       gx+=2
     else
       if diff>mhigh then
         gy+=(16-diff)
       gx+=2
       end
     end
   else
     dx=0
   end
end

if dy==-2 then
   if checkit(gx,gy)==3 then
```

```
        diff=gx % 16
        if diff<mlow then
          gx-=diff
          gy-=2
        else
          if diff>mhigh then
            gx+=(16-diff)
        gy-=2
          end
        end
      else
        dy=0
      end
    end


  if dy==2 then
    if checkit(gx,gy+1)==3 then
      diff=gx % 16
      if diff<mlow then
        gx-=diff
        gy+=2
      else
        if diff>mhigh then
          gx+=(16-diff)
        gy+=2
        end
      end
    else
      dy=0
    end
  end

  if checkit(gx-8,gy+1)==4 then
    for r=1,11,1 do
      gy+=16
      if checkit(gx-8,gy+1)==1 or checkit(gx-8,gy+1)==3 then
        break
      end
      if gy>=223 then
```

```lua
        break
      end
    end
  end

  if gy>=223 then
    lives-=1
    if lives==0 then
      gamend()
    end

    s:playNote(110)
    s:noteOff()
    resetpizza()
  end
  if px<16 then px=16 end
  if px>368 then px=368 end
  if py<16 then py=16 end
  if py>208 then py=208 end
  pizzaction()
end

-- ***********************************************
function gamend()
  gfx.drawText("Game Over.  Press A to restart.",100,40)
  gamestate=0
end

-- ***********************************************
function playdate.AButtonDown()
  lives=5
  score=0

  px=192
  py=144
  gx=192
  gy=208
  initlevel()
  gamestate=1
  ex={92,292}
```

```
    ey={1,1}
    gfx.clear()
    tilemap:setTiles(aa, 126)
  end


  --  ************************************************
  function playdate.update()
    if gamestate==0 then
      return
    end

    if playdate.buttonIsPressed(playdate.kButtonUp) or
      playdate.buttonIsPressed(playdate.kButtonDown) or
      playdate.buttonIsPressed(playdate.kButtonLeft) or
      playdate.buttonIsPressed(playdate.kButtonRight) then

      pizzamove()
    end

    enemymove()
    tilemap:draw(0,64,gx,0,399,176)
    pizzaimg:draw(192,gy)
    enemyimg:draw(ex[1],ey[1])
    enemyimg1:draw(ex[2],ey[2])

    gfx.setColor(gfx.kColorWhite)
    gfx.fillRect(0,0,399,32)
    gfx.setColor(gfx.kColorBlack)
    gfx.drawText("gold="..score,0,0)
    gfx.drawText("lives="..lives,350,0)
  end
```

Program 14 - Hitomezashi patterns

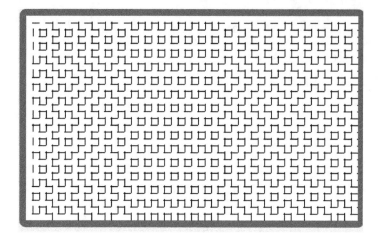

The Hitomezashi algorithm draws a random maze-like pattern.

When drawing vertical lines across the screen, they are randomly either drawn from the top of the screen or offset by the blocksize.

When drawing horizontal lines down the screen, they are randomly either drawn from the left side of the screen or offset by the blocksize.

Press the A button to draw another pattern. Nothing is needed in the playdate.update() function.

```
--hitomezashi pattern
--this implementation copyright 2024 R. Tanikawa

import 'CoreLibs/sprites.lua'
import 'CoreLibs/graphics.lua'
import 'CoreLibs/crank'
import 'CoreLibs/timer'

gfx = playdate.graphics

--********************************

function hito()
```

```
    s=8
    for y=s,232,s do
      i=s*math.random(2)-1
      for x=i,400,2*s do
        gfx.drawLine(x,y,x+s,y)
      end
    end
    for x=s,400,s do
      i=s*math.random(2)-1
      for y=i,232,2*s do
        gfx.drawLine(x,y,x,y+s)
      end
    end
end

hito()

--************************************

function playdate.AButtonDown()
  gfx.clear()
  hito()
end

function playdate.update()

end
```

Program 15 - Maze generator

To make a maze, we randomly pick whether to fill a square to the left or up from "pillars" starting at the upper left. Depending on which corner we start from, we randomly fill a square from a "pillar" in either direction toward that corner.

X	X	X	X	X	X	X
X		1				X
X		O		O	2	X
X						X
X		O		O	3	X
X		4				X
X	X	X	X	X	X	X

If WX and WY are the wall coordinates, PX and PY are the pillar coordinates, and Z is a variable that is either 0 or 1, then we can use the following equations:

WX=PX-Z
WY=PY-1+Z

When Z=0, WX=PX and WY=PY-1, and we make a wall above the pillar (number 1 in the chart above).

If Z=1, then WX=PX-1 and WY=PY, and we would make a wall to the left of the pillar.

Press the A button to make another maze. Again, nothing is needed in the
playdate.update() function.

```lua
--maze generator
--copyright 2024 R. Tanikawa

import 'CoreLibs/sprites.lua'
import 'CoreLibs/graphics.lua'
import 'CoreLibs/crank'
import 'CoreLibs/timer'

gfx = playdate.graphics
local spritelib = gfx.sprite


--*********************************

function maze()
  gfx.fillRect(93,8,217,217)
  gfx.setColor(gfx.kColorWhite)
  gfx.fillRect(100,15,203,203)

  gfx.fillRect(100,8,7,7)
  gfx.fillRect(296,218,7,7)
  gfx.setColor(gfx.kColorBlack)
  i=2
  j=2
  bsize=7
  while i<30 do
    while j<30 do
      gfx.fillRect(93+i*bsize,8+j*bsize,bsize,bsize)
      j+=2
    end
    j=2
    i+=2
  end
  i=2
  j=0

  while j<14 do
    while i<(28-j*2) do
```

```
      z=math.random(2)-1
      gfx.fillRect(93+(i+1-z+j)*bsize,8+(2-z+j)*bsize,bsize,bsize)
      z=math.random(2)-1
      gfx.fillRect(93+(28+z-j)*bsize,8+(i+1-z+j)*bsize,bsize,bsize)
      z=math.random(2)-1
      gfx.fillRect(93+(i+1+z+j)*bsize,8+(28+z-j)*bsize,bsize,bsize)
      z=math.random(2)-1
      gfx.fillRect(93+(2-z+j)*bsize,8+(i+1+z+j)*bsize,bsize,bsize)
      i+=2
    end
    j+=2
    i=2
  end
end


maze()

--***********************************

function playdate.AButtonDown()
  gfx.clear()
  maze()
end

--***********************************

function playdate.update()

end
```

Sideloading Programs

There are 2 ways to sideload programs on the Panic Playdate. Of course, you would want to make sure that the program works in the simulator before loading it into the Playdate hardware.

Sideloading using the USB port

The easiest way is to connect the Playdate to your computer's USB port. On the Playdate, press the upper right menu button and go to Settings, and select System. Then select Reboot to Data Disk. On your computer, you will see a PLAYDATE drive in your Finder (on Mac) or Windows Explorer. Go to the location of your programs .PDX file and copy it (Ctrl-C on Windows, or Cmd-C on Mac). Then go to the PLAYDATE drive and go to the Games folder and then the User folder. Here you paste your .PDX program (Ctrl-V on Windows, or Cmd-V on Mac). Then eject the PLAYDATE drive.

Sideloading using the Playdate website

Go to the website play.date and log into your account. Click on Account and the Sideload. Click on Choose a File and select your .PDX program file.

It is possible that if your .PDX file is large, The file may fail to load or install (the result of compiling many builds of your project), you may have to do some cleanup.

Here are 2 ways I found.

1. Each compile of a program seems to make another subdirectory of your program.PDX file. So if you delete the .PDX file, when you compile the program with pdc, it will make a fresh .PDX file (which is actually a directory).

2. If deleting the .PDX file doesn't fix the problem, you may have to make a new directory with your .lua file or files, the pdxinfo file and any images or sounds in a SystemAssets subdirectory.